BOOK OF

Chili

BOOK OF
Chili

JACKIE FRENCH

Angus&Robertson
An imprint of HarperCollins*Publishers*

Cover: Ornamental chili peppers. Admire ornamental
chili peppers for their beauty, but do not attempt to
eat them. They are toxic.

An Angus & Robertson Publication

Angus&Robertson, an imprint of
HarperCollins*Publishers*
25 Ryde Road, Pymble, Sydney NSW 2073, Australia
31 View Road, Glenfield, Auckland 10, New Zealand
Distributed in the US by HarperCollins*Publishers*
10 East 53rd Street, New York NY 10022, USA

First published in Australia in 1994

Quote on page 24 from Popul Vuh
Copyright © 1985 by Dennis Tedlock
Reprinted by permission of Simon & Schuster

No Library of Congress Cataloging Publication Data
available at the time of printing.

ISBN 0 207 18544 1.

Printed in Hong Kong
9 8 7 6 5 4 3 2 1
97 96 95 94

CONTENTS

CHILI

ADDICTIVE CHILI PEPPER

Peter Piper picked a peck of pickled pepper;
A peck of pickled pepper Peter Piper picked;
If Peter Piper picked a peck of pickled pepper,
Where's the peck of pickled pepper that Peter Piper picked?

Chili pepper is not a subtle food — though it can be used with subtlety.
It will grab you by the taste buds, bite you, burn you, blister you, and
leave you panting. When the flames have died away,
you'll long for more.

Chili pepper has been called the "yuppie food," loved by "foodies"
jaded with less strident tastes. Capsaicin, which gives chili pepper its
fire, doesn't taste of anything itself. It accentuates other flavors, and
makes them much more vivid, even when its fire is barely detectable.
This of course is one of the chili pepper's great attractions for the
cuisines of less affluent countries — it disguises or lifts limited
ingredients. Chili pepper is the food of poverty as well as plenty.

The more capsaicin a chili pepper contains, the more 'bite' it has. Capsaicin content is measured on a scale of 1–120. Common red bird's eye chili peppers rate about 15. (Some chili peppers can be very hot indeed.) Capsaicin triggers the trigeminal nerve, which has branches in the eyes, nose, tongue, and mouth. When you eat a large dose of chili pepper, you don't just experience a flavor hit and a burning sensation — your eyes and nose may water too, and your throat feel like it's about to close up.

Small amounts of chili pepper can provoke a quite different reaction. Chili is used in an enormous range of prepared foods, not necessarily to give fieriness, but just as a slight 'bite' to accentuate other flavors or to make bland food more interesting. Scientific tests in Australia have shown that capsaicin, in any amount at body or room temperature, increases the overall intensity or strength of sugary or salty solutions. As capsaicin doesn't activate the taste buds, this increased flavor impact may be because chili pepper triggers the release of endorphins, the natural morphines that create a feeling of pleasure — so the food is more pleasurable too.

Chili pepper has also been widely used medicinally. Contrary to folklore, it doesn't irritate the stomach lining and can, in fact, help stomach ulcers. Chili pepper is excellent in low salt or sugar diets — it gives food pungency without harmful side effects. So eat them and enjoy.

Chili peppers are high in protein — they contain about 3 percent — though it's unlikely that you'll eat enough of them to make a major addition to the protein in your diet. The capsaicin in chili pepper

Okra Soup

SERVES 4

~ 6 cups chicken or fish stock
~ 6 okra buds, thinly sliced
~ 2 fresh red chili peppers, chopped and seeded
~ 2 bay leaves
~ 1 tbspn fresh parsley, chopped
~ 1 tspn fresh coriander, chopped
~ 1 tbspn fresh chives, chopped

Simmer the stock, okra, chili peppers, and bay leaves for ½ hour. Remove the bay leaves. Serve hot with the herbs sprinkled on top.

Chili Almonds

Sizzle chili powder in hot oil, then sauté almonds till golden brown. Serve hot — in more ways than one.

Chicken and Coriander Soup

✿✿

SERVES 4

~ 1 tbspn scallions (white part only), finely chopped
~ 2 fresh red chili peppers, chopped and seeded
~ 4 cups good chicken stock
~ 4 button mushrooms, thinly sliced
~ 1 tbspn raw or cooked chicken, chopped
~ 1 tbspn fresh coriander, chopped

Add the scallions and chili pepper to the stock and bring to the boil. Add mushrooms, bring to the boil again, then throw in the chicken and coriander. (If using raw chicken, add it at the same time as the chili.) Take off the heat at once and serve hot.

Note: This is a clear and delicate — if fiery — soup. Its success depends on all ingredients being as finely chopped as possible.

also increases the metabolic rate, supposedly helping weight loss. Unfortunately, even a diet high in chili pepper will only increase your metabolism by about 3 percent — enough perhaps for an extra apple a day. Chili peppers may cool you down as well as warm you up — the more you sweat, the more moisture will evaporate, especially if there is a breeze, and the cooler you'll feel.

Chili pepper has been used to repel garden pests, to stop barnacles attaching themselves to boats, as an aphrodisiac, as a cure for sore throats and varicose ulcers, as an antidote to alcoholism, and by a West Indian tribe to torture their captives. (I won't go into details.) It was also used by the Aztecs to punish young girls for sexual immorality.

Chili peppers are possibly addictive — the body gets used to the buzz from increased endorphin levels. So beware. A touch of Tabasco sauce in your tomato juice may seem harmless today — but tomorrow you may be led to the depravities of Thai curry, chili on your pizza, or chili con carne.

THE HISTORY OF CHILI PEPPER

*I have not yet made up my mind to endure some dishes, such as the chili,
but pulque can be sipped 'à discretion'.*

~

FANNY CALDERON DE LA BARCA, WIFE OF THE SPANISH AMBASSADOR TO MEXICO, 1839

Chili peppers are American solanums, from the same family as tomatoes,
eggplants, and tobacco. It is uncertain whether they originated in
Mexico and spread south, or in South America, around Bolivia, and
spread north. Wild chili peppers were possibly eaten in Mexico from as
early as 7000 B.C., and by 5000 B.C. they were being cultivated.

In South America chili peppers have been grown since at least 2500
B.C. — not just the slender red or green chili peppers we are familiar
with, but an enormous range of shapes, colors, tastes, and heat. They
were also used as a form of currency.

Christopher Columbus named the chili pepper 'pepper' at the same
time he called the inhabitants of the West Indies, Indians. Both names
were a mistake — he'd neither reached India nor found true pepper —
but both have stuck. Europe's first taste of chili pepper was collected
from the island of Hispaniola in the West Indies. The Hispaniolans had
obtained their chili peppers from the upper Orinoco region of what is
now Venezuela, in South America.

Hot Orange and Chili Scallop Salad

SERVES 4

~ 24 scallops
~ 2 tbspns olive oil
~ 4 small fresh red chili peppers, finely chopped
~ juice of 1 lime or lemon
~ juice of 1 orange
~ zest of 2 oranges, finely grated
~ green and red lettuce leaves

Heat a little of the oil in a skillet until it is as hot as possible. Drop the scallops in three at a time, fry quickly on one side until just brown, then fry on the other side. Remove the scallops and keep warm in a bowl. Place the chili, juices, zest, and the remaining oil in the skillet and allow to bubble at the highest possible heat until the sauce amalgamates — about 2 minutes. Place the scallops on the lettuce leaves and pour the hot sauce over them. Serve at once.

It is a pity that Columbus or his physician didn't think to feed a little of this new plant to their sailors on the journey home. Chili pepper is higher in vitamin C than orange juice, and may have prevented the sailors dying from scurvy.

Columbus himself wasn't particularly interested in chili peppers or sweet peppers — he was after black pepper, cinnamon and nutmeg. Doctor Alvarez Chanca, the expedition's medico, was more curious, though from a medicinal rather than a culinary point of view. He was the one who introduced the chili pepper to Ecille, in Spain, from where it spread rapidly, being regarded as a new form of "pepper" — hotter and stronger than the "Caucasian" type, as the more familiar white or black pepper was then known. (In Spain the heat was gradually bred out of chili peppers — they became bigger, lusher, and sweeter.)

Like potatoes, chili and sweet peppers were first grown in Europe mostly as ornamentals in the gardens of the aristocracy, but unlike potatoes, their culinary possibilities began to spread, particularly in the Mediterranean, within decades of their introduction to Spain. Chili pepper was one of the few New World spices that would grow in Europe — though admittedly only as an annual, and even then with difficulty. (In fact chili pepper is a fruit, not a spice — but it is certainly spicy.)

It so suited the 15th century palate that many gardeners or their employers were prepared to go to almost any lengths to grow fresh chili pepper. And of course dried chili pepper continued to be a major export from warmer areas around the Mediterranean to the colder parts of Europe.

Chili pepper spread from the Mediterranean to Central Europe, where it metamorphosed into paprika. It reached the Philippines early in the 1500s, and from there it traveled to India, Southeast Asia (where it was accepted with gusto), and China soon after. The Chinese provinces of Hunan and Szechuan are now noted for their extremely spicy and chili-enriched dishes.

Szechuan scholars sometimes claim that the Chinese were the first to cultivate chili peppers (along with apricots and kiwi fruit). Indian culinary historians sometimes claim the same thing, describing with corroborative detail how chili pepper first grew wild on an island in the Indian Ocean. There is no record, however, of chili peppers occurring in either country before Columbus's voyage, though other "peppers" were in use. According to Clusius in his *Exoticorum* (1605), chili pepper was first cultivated in India under the name of Pernambuco pepper. It is likely that if chili pepper were known in China before Columbus

Marinated Sardine and Chili Salad

SERVES 4

~ 12 sardines, freshly broiled or canned in good oil

~ 3 fresh red chili peppers, chopped

~ 4 tbspns olive oil

~ 1 tbspn lime or lemon juice

~ ¼ tspn lime or lemon zest, grated

~ ½ red sweet pepper, thinly sliced

~ 1 tspn fresh parsley, chopped

~ 1 tspn white or Spanish onion, grated

~ 1 tspn fresh oregano, chopped

~ 4 large, very ripe, red tomatoes or 8 fragrant egg tomatoes, chopped

Mix all ingredients except the tomatoes. Leave to marinate overnight. Add the tomatoes just before serving.

Chili and Olive Pizza

≈∽𝒪𝓃

SERVES 4

~ 1 pizza base
~ 2 tspns olive oil
~ 1 cup ripe tomato, puréed
~ 1 cup black olives, pitted
~ 8 fresh red chili peppers
(preferably Jalapeño)
~ chunks of Bocconcini cheese
(not grated) or other fresh
cheese

Brush the pizza base with
oil, spread with the tomato,
then scatter the olives, chili
pepper, and cheese chunks
over it. Bake in as hot an
oven as possible for about
10 minutes, until the edges
of the base are brown. Serve
at once, very hot.

(it almost certainly wasn't known in India), it
would have reached Asia from South America,
rather than originating there.

Chili pepper arrived in England about 1548,
where, according to Gerard in *The Herball or
Historie of Plants* (1597), it was "veery well knowne
in the shoppes at Billingsgate by the name of
Ginnie pepper." It was both eaten and used
medicinally. Gerard described it as "extreme hot
and dry, even in the fourth degree," and
recommended it as a cure for the King's Evil,
or scrofula, a common skin, throat, and lymphatic
infection. However, Evelyn, in his *Acetaria,
a Discourse of Sallets* (1699), described it as "of
dangerous consequence with us; being so much
more acrimonious and terribly biting quality."

In Victorian England chili pepper was
particularly prized for its "warming properties" in
treating arthritis, chills, rheumatism, sprains, and
depression. In the 20th century Mrs C. F. Lyel,
in her *Herbal Delights* (1937), recommended it to
dilate the blood vessels of alcoholics — a remedy
not to be relied upon.

Since chili peppers and sweet peppers were
introduced to Europe by Columbus, they have
evolved into thousands of varieties and cultivars.
Chili pepper is perhaps the most widely grown
of all spices, adapted to every major cuisine from
India, China, Africa, the Middle East, Japan, the
Mediterranean, Southeast Asia, and most parts of
Europe, either in its most fiery form or as a touch
of spicy piquancy in a few grains of cayenne pepper.
The United States imports over 80 million lb of hot
chili pepper every year.

WHICH CHILI PEPPER?

Some hold there are but two sorts of Chiles or Chilli, the one the Eastern which is Ginger, and the other Western, which is the Pepper of Mexico.

~

EDWARD CHAMBERLAYNE, *COFFEE, TEA AND CHOCOLATE*, 1685

A chili pepper is a member of the *Capsicum* genus. The word "capsicum" may be derived from the Greek "kapto," to bite. An alternative derivation has it coming from the Latin "capsa" or "capio," meaning to hold — the same derivation as capsule.

There are five main species of plants producing chili peppers, with hundreds of varieties. Over 100 are found in Mexico alone, with many being specific to a particular region. Some Mexican chili peppers are almost solely for drying, others are usually used fresh. New varieties have been developed in almost every area in which chilies are grown, and new commercial varieties are introduced each year.

Capsicum annuum

This is the most commonly grown of the Western *Capsicum* species. Most of the varieties in this species are mild or at most spicy sweet peppers, rather than fiery chili peppers. *C. annuum* grows to about 2⅔ ft tall, with white flowers and pungent, drooping, tapered fruit growing up to 1 ft long. *C. annuum* has only one fruit emerging from each growing point, and is best grown in temperate areas. "Annuum" is Latin for annual, and most peppers are grown as annuals, though in frost-free areas they may survive for two seasons if the fruit is picked regularly.

Grilled Peaches with Chili

𝒶𝒷𝓃

SERVES 4

~ 4 red chili peppers or a dash of Tabasco sauce, Chili Sherry (page 23), or other chili sauce (not dried chili peppers or chili powder)
~ 4 firm peaches
~ 4 tspns packed brown sugar

If using chili peppers, chop as finely as possible. Cut peaches into halves, place under a broiler, and sprinkle a little chili and sugar over each. Cook until the sugar dissolves and bubbles. Serve very hot.

Cayenne chili pepper

Capsicum frutescens

This species produces the hottest chili peppers, including devil's chili peppers. It is usually grown as a perennial up to 6 ft tall, though it can be grown as an annual in cooler areas, with woody stems and greenish-white flowers. Two or three fruit grow from each node. The fruit varies from red to yellow to orange, in a range of shapes. It is grown extensively in India, Japan, China, Mexico, Turkey, and Africa.

C. chinense is now classified as a form of *C. frutescens*, which will cross with *C. annuum* — so take care with any seed you plant. Your mild sweet pepper may turn into a savage, blistering beast.

Capsicum pubescens

Also known as or hairy sweet pepper or Manzano chili pepper, this was a popular Inca chili. It grows for at least ten years and is perhaps the most cold-tolerant of all the hot chili peppers. It will also survive high altitudes, and does not hybridize with other species. It has bluish-purple flowers, small, oblong, pointed, pungent fruits in red or orange, black seeds, and slightly fuzzy leaves.

14
~

Capsicum pendulum

From Ecuador, Peru, and Bolivia, it has conical, pungent fruits and yellow or brown spotted flowers.

Capsicum baccatum

This is an incredibly hot fruit, with large flowers and leaves. It is a species that includes the Central American Escabeche chili pepper, much used in Mexican cookery, and the Andean Aji, cultivated for at least 4000 years.

Other Chili Pepper Varieties

There are too many chili pepper varieties to list here. The best known commercially available ones include Jalapeño, cayenne, and Chilitepine peppers. Chilitepines are also called bird's eye chilies, and unlike most hot chili peppers, are a variety of *C. annuum*. Bird's eye chilies still grow wild in Central America and Mexico, as well as being cultivated.

Jalapeño chili peppers are hot Mexican chilies, not quite as blazing as bird's eye chilies, with thick-fleshed fruit that grow to about 3 in. long. They are one of the best pizza chili peppers — hot enough to singe your tongue, but not powerful enough to do serious damage. Cayenne chili peppers are slim, red, and sweet, hot but not too fiery.

Lipstick chili peppers are slim, sweet, and conical, about 5 in. long — a good variety for short, cool summers. They have more flavor than some of the hotter chili peppers, and work well with chicken or other delicate dishes, where you want sweetness and taste as well as heat.

Jalapeño chili pepper

Chili Antipasto

Place whole red or green chili peppers in a glass jar, along with layers of any or all of the following: sun-dried tomatoes, dried eggplant, black, green or stuffed olives, chunks of fetta, Bocconcini, mozzarella or any other smooth, close-textured cheese, garlic cloves, strips of lemon peel (with absolutely no white), and artichoke hearts. Pour in olive oil, making sure that it completely covers the other ingredients. Seal and marinate in a cool, dark place for at least 2 weeks.

Hot Spiced Olives

Combine good olives with whole or chopped chili peppers, a few sprigs of fresh thyme or oregano, and cover with olive oil. Leave for at least 2 weeks to marinate.

Anaheim chili peppers have tapered, deep green to partially red fruit that are moderately hot and grow to 8 in. long. Hungarian hot wax chili peppers are waxy yellow, tapered fruits, 6 in. long, hot but not fiery, and not to be confused with sweet banana peppers — long, sweet, yellow fruit that change to orange-red when ripe, and aren't hot at all. Hungarian hot wax chili peppers are good in long-cooking vegetable or beef stews, and their sweetness marries well with a touch of lemon juice or dairy sour cream.

Habañero chili peppers are orange-yellow, about 1½–2½ in. long, and five times hotter than bird's eyes. Pick them with gloves on. Serrano chili peppers are a good commercial variety, turning from deep green to fire red when ripe, but equally pungent at either stage. Long red cayenne is a sweet, hot chili pepper, about 5 in. long. It is excellent for sauces and chutneys, as its flavor is not overpowered by its fire.

Other chili peppers include Thai hot, black, Bombay red, devil, Californian, fiesta, and fire fly.

How to Grow Chili Pepper

Chili peppers tolerate cold weather so long as it is not frosty, even though they may stop fruiting. They are usually grown as an annual in frosty areas.

Alternatively, they can be kept indoors until the frosts are over, provided they are frequently taken out into the sunlight on balmy days. In warmer areas that have few frosts, they can be covered during winter.

In frost-free, temperate to tropical areas, most chili peppers are short-lived perennials. With care, they will bear fruit for up to ten years, or longer if they are kept well fed and pruned once or twice a season. New wood is hardier, more vigorous, and less likely to break down with cool or humid weather.

Chili peppers tolerate almost any soil, but like most plants, do best on fertile, well-drained, moist loam that is slightly acidic. They need plenty of sun and at least four to six hot sunny months to produce a good mature crop. In cooler areas your chili peppers may not mature — though they can still be used — or the plants may produce one flush of chili peppers instead of several.

Hot Pickled Cucumbers

~ a little salt

~ 4 European or other soft-skinned cucumbers, sliced and seeded but not peeled

~ 2 cups white wine vinegar

~ 3 tbspns white or raw sugar

~ 2 fresh red or green chili peppers, chopped

Sprinkle salt on the cucumbers and place in a bowl. Leave for 2 hours, then pour off any liquid. Make sure the cucumbers are as well drained as possible. Boil the vinegar and sugar, stirring until the sugar dissolves, then pour over the cucumbers. Add the chili peppers and bring to the boil, then remove from the heat at once. Bottle and seal.

The cucumbers can be eaten as soon as they are cool or left for up to a month in a cool, dark place. Refrigerate once opened.

Chili peppers need temperatures of at least 65°F to germinate. Plant your chili seed when the soil no longer feels cold — insert a finger to test this. In cooler areas where chili peppers need lots of sun to fruit, plant established seedlings about 16 in. apart (10 in. apart in warmer areas). Plant the seedlings fairly deep and water well in dry times.

Only water the base if possible, not the fruit or flowers.

Chili pepper seed germinates in about five to ten days, but may remain dormant for up to eight weeks in cold soil. Like tomato seed, chili seed rarely rots if planted too early or even if left in the soil over winter from last year's plants. Seedlings that spring up too early, however, will be cut by late frosts.

Keep your plants weed-free until they are well established.

The more you pick your chili peppers, the more the bush will produce, as it will not have to put energy into seed production. Mature chili peppers, however, have a better taste and store longer.

If your chili peppers die down after a light frost or cold winter, simply cut them back to ground level. If the soil has not been too cold, they may shoot again in spring — though they will be slow to produce and newly planted seedlings will possibly bear before they do.

Stake chili pepper plants in windy areas as they are shallow-rooted and can topple over.

HARVESTING YOUR OWN CHILI PEPPER SEED

Some particularly delicious or hot varieties of chili peppers can be hard to come by. Keeping your own seed is a way of ensuring supply — and also of making sure that rare varieties survive.

Chili peppers are self-pollinating, but can be pollinated by insects, and when this happens one variety can "cross" with another nearby variety. Chili pepper pollen is dominant over sweet pepper pollen. If you grow chili peppers next to sweet peppers, take care when crunching into next year's crop — the formerly mild sweet peppers may sear your tongue.

As with all seed collecting, select the most vigorous plant that gives the best tasting chili peppers from which to harvest seed. You can also breed for the qualities you find most desirable — early fruiting, late fruiting, frost or cold tolerance, particularly plump or sweet or hot fruit, or fruit with tough skins that resist fruit fly.

Cloak the bushes in shade cloth, or place nylon stockings strung over coat-hanger wires over the whole plant, or at least over one flowering branch, to stop insects approaching. This will ensure that each bush pollinates itself.

Chili and Garlic Bread

SERVES 4

~ 8 oz butter
~ 10 garlic cloves, crushed
~ 3 red chili peppers, finely chopped and seeded
~ 1 tbspn fresh parsley, finely chopped
~ 1 tbspn fresh chives, finely chopped
~ 1 French bread stick, cut into slices diagonally

Beat the butter with the garlic, chili peppers, and herbs until light. Spread generous spoonfuls in between each slice of bread. Wrap in aluminum foil or simply place in the center of an oven preheated to 400°–500°F. Leave for 5–10 minutes, or until the butter has melted between each slice. Serve hot.

Hot Peanut Sauce

Excellent with anything fried or broiled, or with steamed or baked potatoes. It will last for a week in the refrigerator.

~ *2 cups raw peanuts or 1 cup crunchy peanut butter (raw peanuts give a better result)*

~ *4 tbspns peanut oil*

~ *juice of 3 limes or lemons*

~ *2 fresh chili peppers (preferably Thai), chopped*

~ *1 tbspn tomato purée (optional)*

~ *a little brown sugar (optional, and certainly not needed if you are using peanut butter)*

Fry the raw peanuts until browned in a little of the oil, or place them on a baking sheet and brown them in the oven. Place all ingredients in a blender and turn it on for a few "pulses" — just enough to mix together, not to make it smooth and unctuous. If you are using peanut butter, a good mixing by hand is all that is needed. Taste, and add salt if necessary.

After the bush has fruited, pick the chili peppers. Scrape the seeds out and dry them well in full sunlight. If you are collecting large amounts of seed, place the whole ripe fruit in a blender with twice the quantity of water and blend for a few seconds at low speed. Let the red mash settle for 1 hour. The seeds should rise to the top. Scoop them out and dry them on newspaper. As always when working with chili peppers, wear gloves and work in a well-ventilated room if you are using large quantities.

Chili pepper seeds are viable for about five years. (I store mine in old envelopes in a cupboard.) After that they may still germinate — and often those that do germinate will be tough, hardy plants — but be prepared for a lot of the seed to fail.

I have grown chili peppers by scraping the seeds from commercially dried chilies and planting them, but this procedure is risky as the chili peppers may be too old to germinate, they may have been heat-treated so that they are no longer viable, or they may introduce disease. However, if you find a particularly good dried chili pepper, you may like to try it.

PROBLEMS WITH GROWING CHILI PEPPERS

Leaf Spots

Leaf spots are worse in hot, humid conditions or if the plant is old, and does not have a great deal of new growth. Feed chili plants well with compost or a good mulch combined with a little blood and bone or hen manure. Do this at least twice during the growing season.

In bad cases spray the plants with a copper sulfate spray if the temperature is under 74°F. Don't spray flowers or fruit as you may damage them. Regular seaweed or compost sprays (made by covering compost or seaweed with water, ready to use when it is the color of weak tea) may give some resistance. In very bad cases mulch with weed mat or newspaper to stop spores splashing up onto the leaves.

Fruit Fly

Blistered, rotting skin or small white maggots inside fruit are symptoms of fruit fly infection. This should only be a problem if fruit flies are extremely bad in your area — chili peppers have relatively thick skins and fruit flies attack tomatoes and other fruit before they will spread to them.

In areas with a severe infestation of fruit fly, make sure ALL fallen fruit is picked up the same day it falls and that no fruit flies are breeding in smelly rubbish heaps masquerading as compost.

You can also try fruit fly repellent. It keeps away small numbers of fruit fly — as well as dogs, cats, and Aunt Maud, who has come to smell the flowers.

Chili Noodles

SERVES 4

~ 4 tbspns olive or peanut oil
~ 3 fresh red chili peppers (preferably Jalapeño), chopped and seeded
~ 4 leeks (white part only), chopped
~ 1 green and 2 red sweet peppers, sliced in long thin strips
~ 4 garlic cloves, chopped
~ ½ cup peanuts or macadamia nuts, chopped
~ 1 tspn dark soy sauce
~ 3 cups noodles, cooked

Heat the oil and fry the chili peppers, leeks, sweet peppers, garlic, and nuts until the leeks are cooked. Add the soy sauce, then quickly stir in the noodles. Cook only until the noodles are hot. Serve at once.

Sweet Chili Sauce

~ 20 fresh red chili peppers
~ 1 cup distilled white
vinegar
~ ½ cup water
~ 4 cloves garlic

*Put all ingredients in a pot
and simmer until the chili
peppers are cooked — about
10 minutes. Keep the lid on
and do not inhale the fumes.
If you do, you will be sorry.
Remove from the heat and
cool — this is important
because if you blend chili
peppers while they are hot,
you will gag or blister on the
fumes. Now process in a
blender until smooth. Bottle
at once. Keep in the
refrigerator and use a little
— a very little — as
needed.*

The smell is overpowering. It's not "organic"
either. Don't spill any on your skin.

Mix 4 cups kerosene, 4 cups creosote, and
1 package of mothballs. Place it in cans and either
hang the cans from fruit trees about 11 yds apart, or
set them at 4½-yd intervals in the vegetable garden.
If you can't smell it, you possibly need more cans.
Mothballs by themselves have a limited repellent
value against fruit fly. Hang garlands of them
between your chili bushes. (I must stress that the
effect is limited — simply hanging mothballs in
your branches won't cure your fruit fly problem.)

As a last resort use a commercial, splash-on
product that combines a protein hydrolysate bait
with maldison. This certainly isn't organic — but
as the bait can be splashed onto the leaves or stem,
rather than sprayed through the chili peppers
themselves, the effect on you and the surroundings
is limited. I recommend it in bad fruit fly areas
where you can't control "other people's fruit flies"
zeroing in on you.

Rotten Fruit

Chili peppers will rot if they are damaged in any way on the plant — whether by fruit fly, slugs, snails, overeager grasshoppers (chili peppers are one of the last fruits grasshoppers will attack), frost or hail damage, or mechanical damage from spades or other tools. Chili peppers may also rot in hot, humid conditions. A copper sulfate spray or other fungicide can be applied according to the manufacturer's directions to stop this happening.

Chili Sherry

This is delicious, simple to make, and tastes much better than Tabasco sauce. Add a few drops to anything you want to imbue with a touch of fire.

Fill a jar with fresh chili peppers — dried chili peppers can be substituted but fresh have more flavor. Cover with sherry, either sweet or dry, depending on whether you prefer a sweet or dry sauce. You can substitute whisky, which also makes an excellent sauce. Chili Sherry gets hotter as it ages. Two-year-old Chili Sherry would give a dragon a blistered tongue; but it is usually too good to last that long.

Spiced Chili Sherry

Add a few cumin seeds, cardamom pods, and a little fresh, chopped ginger to Chili Sherry (above). A few drops — no more — are a good addition to plain chicken or beef bouillon, or add to a light cream sauce served with broiled fish or chicken or steamed vegetables.

HARVESTING AND STORING CHILI PEPPER

When the rat had named it, they gave the rat his food, and this is his food: corn kernels, squash seeds, chili, beans, patoxte, cacao. These are his.

~

POPOL VUH

HARVESTING CHILI PEPPERS

The fruit of the chili pepper plant can be harvested at any time. They are fiery as soon as they emerge from the flower. However, mature chili peppers keep better, are much hotter and usually sweeter, with a better flavor. Mature chili peppers are also better for drying, as their skins are tougher and they are less likely to rot. All chili peppers need long periods of sun to ripen — those produced during cool, cloudy seasons lack bite and flavor.

STORING FRESH CHILI PEPPERS

Never store chili peppers with other fruit such as oranges — they will continue to "ripen" and quickly rot. They are best kept in the refrigerator — not in plastic wrap — or in a bowl in a cool dark cupboard. The less moisture, humidity, and heat, the longer your chili peppers will last.

How to Use Fresh Chili Peppers

Simply chop the chili peppers and add to dishes. Very ripe, plump chili peppers are best for this. If they are chopped incredibly finely, you eliminate the danger of chewing unexpectedly on a piece and spending the next half hour gasping.

Try chopped fresh chili peppers:

~ sprinkled on pizza

~ added to bread dough

~ scattered over pasta with a little Parmesan cheese,
chopped basil and olive oil

~ added to salad dressings (chopped very finely)

~ inserted in fish before baking in the oven

~ slipped under the skin of roasting meat, as you would
insert slivers of garlic.

Alternatively, sear the chili peppers under the broiler, turning them when the skin is blackened. Rub off the charred skin under a cold tap. This searing brings out the nutty-sweet flavor and also removes any tough skin.

Mixed Hot Salad

SERVES 4

~ 1 small radicchio lettuce

~ 1 bunch aragula leaves

~ 1 garlic clove, chopped

~ 4 fresh red chili peppers, finely chopped

~ 3 cups goat's cheese or other fresh cheese, in chunks

~ black olives, artichoke hearts, chunks of tuna or salmon, anchovies, sun-dried tomatoes

DRESSING:

~ 4 tbspns olive oil

~ 1 tbspn tarragon or other good vinegar

~ salt and ground black pepper to taste

Mix the dressing. Place other ingredients in a serving bowl and pour the dressing over them. Toss lightly but well — be careful not to break up the fish or artichoke hearts. Serve at once before the radicchio becomes limp.

DRYING CHILI PEPPERS

Leave any chili peppers you want to preserve on the bush until they have withered slightly. In cool or frost-prone areas, dig the plant up, root and all, with as much dirt as possible, before the first frost and hang it under shelter — a shed, garage or verandah is excellent. Let the chili peppers mature on the bush. They will keep growing for at least a month after you dig them up.

When the chili peppers are mature, pick then dry them — in the sun if possible — as fast as you can. Choose a hot, dry day with little cloud cover and a slight breeze. Once dry, store them in an airtight container. Don't pulverize them until you need them for cooking — whole chilies keep their flavor and fire longer than powdered chilies.

Well-dried chili peppers will keep for years, if not decades. (I still have a full jar from 15 years ago — we grew a lot of chili peppers that year. They've lost a little of their potency, but an unwary bite will still paralyze your tongue.)

HOW TO USE DRIED CHILI PEPPERS

Add finely crumbled, dried chili peppers to dishes that need long, moist cooking or marinating. You can either leave the seeds in or remove them. Remember that the seeds are the hottest part, as well as the toughest. For dishes where chili flavor rather than heat is the main requirement, remove the seeds.

Add a few dried chili peppers to dried beans, peas or lentils being soaked overnight. As long as you remove the chili peppers before cooking, they will add zest to an otherwise bland legume dish without adding heat.

Wrap chili peppers in a piece of cloth — cheesecloth or cotton is excellent, old (clean) nylon stockings even better — and add to long-cooking dishes. This is the best method when you want to avoid chewing on a bit of chili pepper later. Remove the bag at the end of the cooking time so no one gets an overly hot mouthful.

Cook chili peppers in a little oil for 5 minutes before adding other ingredients.

Try a little dried chili:

~ added to basic stock to give it greater pungency and reduce the amount of salt needed
~ added to chutneys and pickles
~ used instead of extra salt or sugar in tomato and other sauces.

Burning Steak

SERVES 4

~ 1 tbspn olive oil
~ 4 pieces fillet or sirloin steak
~ 4 fresh chili peppers, chopped and seeded
~ 1 garlic clove, chopped
~ ½ cup brandy, cognac, or whisky

Heat the oil in a skillet until you can see transparent smoke coming from it. Add the steaks and cook on as high a heat as possible until one side is seared, then turn and sear the other side. When they are cooked to your liking, place them on a warmed dish. Throw the chili pepper and garlic into the hot skillet, stir a couple of times to sear, then pour in the alcohol. Allow to bubble furiously, stirring all the time so the juices mingle with the cooking alcohol. Don't worry if it catches alight — the flames will die down as soon as the alcohol is burnt off, and the taste will be even better. After about 1 minute — or once the flames die down — pour the pan juices over the steaks and serve.

Chili Con Carne

SERVES 4–6

~ 1½ lb dried red kidney
beans or 2 lb fresh red
kidney beans

~ 4 tbspns oil

~ 2 lb blade or chuck steak,
chopped

~ 2 onions, chopped

~ 6 garlic cloves, chopped

~ 2 tspns chili powder

~ 1 tbspn all-purpose flour

~ 10 large red tomatoes,
skinned, or 2 x 8 oz cans
of tomatoes

~ 2 tspns oregano

Soak dried beans in water
overnight. Heat oil and sear
the meat, add onion, and stir
until transparent. Add
garlic and chili powder and
cook until garlic is slightly
seared. Add flour, stirring
well so it doesn't become
lumpy. When it is also
slightly browned, add
tomatoes and beans. Simmer
for 1 hour. Add more liquid
only if necessary.

Take off the heat, put a
lid on the saucepan, and
leave in the refrigerator
overnight. Reheat the next
day with the oregano and
cook for a further ½ hour.
Add extra liquid if needed.

COOKING WITH CHILI PEPPER

*'Try a chili with it Miss Sharp', said Joseph, really interested.
'A chili', said Rebecca, gasping; 'oh yes!' She thought a chili
was something cool, as its name imported.*

~

THACKERAY, *VANITY FAIR*, 1853

Chili pepper can be used in cooking in two ways
— stridently, so the dish tastes pungent, hot; or with
extreme discretion, so that the chili pepper simply
accentuates the other flavors. A slight dusting of
cayenne pepper, a few drops of Tabasco sauce or Chili
Sherry (page 23), or a discreet hint of chili in a sauce or
salad dressing can make food infinitely more vivid
without any sensation of "heat" at all. You can even use
chili peppers in desserts, though sparingly. Chili can be
incredibly refreshing — which is what desserts are all
about, and it will also accentuate other flavors if you
want to cut down on the amount of sugar you use.

Almost every cuisine has its own way of using
chili pepper, and many recipes are dependent on the
taste or fieriness of a particular chili variety. Possibly
the most specialized chili usage is in Mexico, where
some recipes specify half a dozen different chili
peppers for one dish. Mexicans inherited part of the
Aztec cuisine, and variations on their chili dishes —
like chili beans and chili con carne — are served
throughout most of the Western world.

One of the most renowned Mexican chili dishes
is Mole Poblano de Guajolte, or turkey in a chili
and chocolate sauce. It was the work of Sister

Andrea de la Asuncion of the convent of Santa Rosa during the 16th century, who created it entirely from imagination, as the members of the convent were forbidden to taste chocolate.

Be warned — even chili peppers from the same plant may vary from mild to tongue blistering. If you are a chili novice, use only small amounts at first, and add more gradually. Dried and ground chili peppers vary greatly in potency, depending on how long and how well they have been stored. When in doubt, be cautious. It is easy to add more heat to a dish. It is almost impossible to remove it.

HOW TO TEST A CHILI PEPPER

Don't just take a bite. You may never crunch again. Cut one end open and rub it on the back of your hand. If it raises a blister, you know you've got a very vicious chili pepper. If it leaves a red mark, you've also got a potent performer. If, however, your hand is unblemished, then — and only then — taste a very little of the end of the chili pepper (not the seeds or membranes) on the middle (not the edges) of your tongue. If you survive you can taste further.

The taste of chili pepper comes from capsaicin, with the color coming from capsanthin and

Chicken Breasts with Chili

SERVES 4

~ 4 chicken breasts, flattened
~ 4 fresh red chili peppers (preferably Jalapeño)
~ 1 tbspn olive oil

SAUCE:

~ 1 cup plain yogurt
~ 1 tbspn fresh coriander, chopped
~ 1 red chili pepper, finely chopped

Mix the ingredients for the sauce together and let it stand.

Insert tiny slivers of the chili into the chicken breasts. Brush a skillet or hotplate with oil and heat as hot as possible, then toss in the chicken. Fry until rich brown, turn over, and cook on the other side. Serve very hot, with a little sauce in the center of each chicken breast.

Chili Pesto

SERVES 4

~ *1 bunch fresh basil leaves*

~ *½ cup pine nuts*

~ *3 fresh red chili peppers*

~ *¼ cup Parmesan cheese, grated*

~ *½ cup olive oil*

~ *juice of ½ lemon or lime*

Blend all ingredients in a blender. Heat in a saucepan to serving temperature and serve over pasta or with good fresh bread. Pesto can be frozen, but will become darker and lose some of the subtleties of flavor.

carotene. Capsaicin is extremely potent — the tiniest speck diluted ten thousandfold can still be tasted. Usually the hotter the chili pepper, the higher the capsaicin content — up to 1 percent of capsaicin, concentrated mainly in the thin membrane where the seeds are attached to the top and center of the flesh. As a very general rule of thumb, the stronger the color, the stronger the taste, though there are many exceptions.

HOW TO TAKE THE BURN OUT OF CHILI PEPPERS

If your mouth is on fire from an inadvertent bite of chili pepper, don't gulp down water. Take a mouthful of rice — or even better, a gulp of milk. The casein (milk protein) will help put out the flames. This is one of the reasons why side dishes of plain yogurt with cucumber or banana are served with Indian and Sri Lankan curries.

If there isn't any milk or plain yogurt on hand, suck a bit of sugar. That will help too.

Always be careful when chopping chili peppers.

30
~

Very hot chili peppers may blister your fingertips or underneath your nails, or you may accidentally rub your eyes or nose. Always wash your hands in warm soapy water, then in salty water with a little vinegar added, as soon as you have finished in case you accidentally scratch yourself. The fumes alone of very potent chili peppers can make your eyes water. I use my son's scuba diving goggles when chopping large amounts. Ski goggles are another good form of protection.

WHAT TO DRINK WITH CHILI PEPPER

Chili pepper will effectively overpower anything you drink with it. When eating chili-laced foods, you drink to help put out the flames, not to appreciate a subtle vintage. A sweetish, late-vintage wine will help you cope with excess heat. Cider, mead, or nonalcoholic sparkling apple juices are also good choices.

Fish in Chili Marinade

SERVES 4

~ 4 whole fish or 8 fish fillets

~ 1 small onion, chopped

~ 1 garlic clove, crushed

~ 2 fresh red chili peppers (preferably Thai), chopped and seeded

~ juice of 1 lemon or lime

~ ½ cup coconut milk

Combine all ingredients, then leave to marinate for at least 2 hours. Remove the fish, dry well, and grill over a very hot fire or fry in a very hot skillet — the fish should char on both sides. Serve with extra lemon juice, or one of the sauces or relishes in this book.

Note: If you leave the fish in this marinade for about 6 hours or overnight, the acid content in the marinade will "cook" the fish, in which case take it out of the marinade and serve it cold and flaked with some shredded lettuce and chopped macadamia nuts.

Chili Powder

Use dried chili peppers that are crisp. If they aren't crisp, dry them a little longer, either in full, hot sunlight or in a very very slow oven. When they crack rather than tear, they are ready.

Put gloves on, then carefully slice each chili pepper open and remove the seeds. Some chili powders contain the seeds too, but these, though often hotter, don't have such a good flavor and may be slightly bitter.

Place the outer skins in a blender and process until powdery. After this first processing they may still be slightly damp. If necessary, spread the powder or lumpy bits onto a sheet of wax paper and dry again, then process again. Adding a little salt or cornstarch may make the processing easier.

Keep chili powder in a dark cupboard, in a sealed jar. If it is quite dry, it will keep for years — especially if salt has been added — but the best flavor will dissipate after a few months, though much of the heat will remain. It is best to make homemade chili powder only in small quantities. Dried whole chili peppers keep their flavor and fire much better.

EXPLOSIVE POWDERS AND FIERY SAUCES

The red powder from the crushed chili pods is pungent, but only for short times. It makes the stomach feel very warm!

~

A HUNGARIAN COUNT, 1793

CHILI POWDER

Chili powder is made from ground red chili peppers. It is quite coarse and should be used where fire rather than delicacy is needed.

The hotness varies depending on the brand, the age of the chili powder, and how well it has been prepared and stored. Unfortunately, the only way to test this is to use it in cooking — with discretion — then add more if needed. Remember that the last bit of chili powder in the container will be a lot milder than the first teaspoon from a new packet. Many a cook has been blistered while using new powder in what they thought was a tried and tested recipe.

Commercial chili powder is rarely pure ground chili pepper. It is usually combined with oregano, cumin, garlic, and other spices, sometimes with flour or other bulking agents also being added.

These may stop the powder from forming damp lumps and ensure that it flows freely.

Chili powder was probably first invented by the Aztecs, though they added native herbs to the ground chili peppers for a quite different flavor. Modern chili powder was invented by a Texan.

Try chili powder:

~ dusted on crackers before baking

~ added to the crumb or flour batter on fried chicken, steak, or in tempura batter

~ dusted over peanuts, almonds etc., then baked in the oven, instead of deep-frying and adding salt

~ a very little bit, added to cheese sauces or soufflés to bring out the flavor.

CAYENNE PEPPER

Cayenne pepper is named after the capital of French Guiana in South America. It can be made from several species of chili pepper, is very finely ground, and usually mixed with flour and salt, so it is soft and powdery. Like chili powder, the actual composition and pungency depends on the brand and how long and how well it has been stored. It is incredibly hot and much finer than chili powder. It is usually added in very small pinches to creamy sauces or sprinkled on crackers where the bite — but not the rich red color — is needed.

Even the best brands of cayenne pepper tend to absorb moisture very quickly. Only small amounts should be bought at any one time. The best cayenne pepper is said to be a rich brown color, rather than red. It can be used in the same ways that I have suggested above for chili powder.

A Very Fine Cayenne Pepper

Take 3 parts dried, seeded chili peppers, and mix with 1 part salt — rock salt is best. Process in the blender until smooth. Add the same quantity of white wine and water, and mix well. Filter, then leave the liquid in the sun until the moisture evaporates. This produces an incredibly fine — and hot — pepper.

Chili Paste

~ 20 fresh or dried chili peppers

~ ½ cup oil

~ ½ cup distilled white vinegar

Simmer all ingredients until the chili peppers are soft and the mixture thick. Bottle, seal tightly, and keep in the refrigerator.

PAPRIKA

Salted Chili Paste

Chop fresh red chili peppers (with gloves on). Place alternate layers of chili pepper and salt in a jar. Each layer should be no more than the thickness of a piece of chili pepper — just thin red and white lines. Seal. The salt will extract the chili juice.

Use small spoonfuls of the paste with discretion. It makes a wonderful coating for a leg of lamb or pork before you roast it. It will make the skin crisp — and fiery — and the gravy drippings will be like caramelized fire as well.

According to legend, a captive harem girl in Budapest in the 17th century discovered a strange bush covered with red fruit in the Turkish garden where she was confined. She smuggled some out to her lover via a secret passage, told him how to sow the seeds — and red peppers, or paprikas, came to be grown in Hungary.

Although this legend is possibly fantasy, it is true that paprika was brought to Europe by the Turks, who called it "paparka."

Paprika is used in an enormous number of dishes, often with dairy sour cream, meat, tomatoes, and garlic. The more seeds and ridges kept during drying, the more coarse and pungent the paprika. The subtlest, most delicate paprika is dried without the seeds or the ridges — it has flavor without so much bite.

Unlike many spices, paprika loses much of its flavor if it is fried at too high a heat. Sear your meat first, then add the paprika while continuing to cook at a lower heat.

Try paprika:

~ in goulash or other stews thick with dairy sour cream
and tomatoes

~ mixed with the dressing on a tomato salad

~ dusted over any cheese dish

~ sprinkled over dairy sour cream on a baked potato

~ added to the crumb batter on fried food

~ added to almost any dish that has a large tomato
or cheese component.

CURRY PASTES AND POWDERS

Until the 16th century, Indian curries relied on
pepper, not chili pepper, for their heat — and
many traditional Indian dishes still avoid the use
of chili, despite the heat of most commercial curry
powders and pastes that are applied liberally in
Western versions of "Indian" cookery.

Curry powders and pastes are best avoided.
You will get better results simply by heating the
individual spices in oil or ghee (clarified butter) at
the start of cooking. However, I have given a recipe
for an all-purpose curry paste for reasons of
convenience — when you only need a little or you
are in a hurry — or to give to friends.

Curry Paste

*The salt in this recipe is
necessary to preserve the
paste. If you must avoid
salt, keep the paste in the
refrigerator, not the
cupboard.*

~ 4 tbspns coriander seeds

~ ½ tbspn cumin seeds

~ 1 tbspn powdered turmeric

~ 1 tspn powdered ginger

~ 1 tbspn salt

~ 4 dried chilies

*~ ½ cup cooking oil (walnut,
peanut, mustard, or safflower
oil are good for this purpose)*

*~ ¼ cup distilled white or
other good vinegar*

*Heat the spices in the oil,
stirring well, for at least
10 minutes, until the scent
fills the kitchen then changes
slightly. This is difficult to
describe, but you will
recognize it when it happens.
Add the vinegar and allow
to bubble until the mixture is
thick. Cool, then blend until
smooth. Pack into small
clean jars and seal.*

Indian Sahib's Sauce

This is a sauce of flames and distinction. It will keep for several months in a cool cupboard. Refrigerate once opened.

~ 4 large onions, chopped

~ 6 tbspns olive oil

~ 1 lb zucchini or marrow

~ 6 garlic cloves, chopped

~ 1 tspn turmeric

~ 20 fresh red chili peppers, chopped

~ 1 tspn cumin

~ 1 tbspn French mustard

Sauté the onion in the oil until transparent. While it is cooking, peel the zucchini or marrow and cut into small pieces. Add the garlic, turmeric, chili peppers, and cumin to the onion and stir well until the scent fills the room. Now add the zucchini or marrow and mustard. Stir frequently until the vegetable is very soft. Take off the heat and mash well. Bottle and seal.

TABASCO SAUCE

Tabasco sauce was invented by ex-merchant banker Ward McIlhenny after he had been bankrupted by the American Civil War. He set up a "chili still" on Avery Island and created Tabasco sauce — one of the most fiery extracts of chili pepper.

The Bloody Mary — reputed hangover cure and general pick-me-up — was invented 55 years later by Fernand Petoit, a bartender at Harry's New York Bar in Paris, from vodka, tomato juice, and Tabasco. The name Bloody Mary was further immortalized by one of the characters in Rodgers and Hammerstein's musical, *South Pacific*. If you prefer an equally fresh but nonalcoholic Virgin Mary, just drink the tomato juice and Tabasco.

Tabasco is an excellent way to add discreet bite to a dish, or to increase the flames at the end of cooking to a dish that has less "oomph" than you expected. A few drops will accentuate the flavor of a dish without adding heat, and is a good way of livening up food, especially if you are on a low salt, low fat, low sugar or otherwise bland diet.

Try any of these suggestions:

~ Sprinkle a few drops over a pizza.

~ Add a dash to stews.

~ The slightest touch in hot chicken soup is incredibly warming.

~ Make a winter drink of hot tomato juice and Tabasco.

~ Stir a little into dips or cheese sauces — not enough to set the dish ablaze, just enough for piquancy.

~ Add 1 drop — no more — to 2 tbspns distilled white vinegar and 4 tbspns olive oil for a piquant vinaigrette.

~ Dribble a little into tomato sauces, or purée fresh tomato with a drop or two.

~ Add the smallest possible amount to cakes, cookies, or other foods where you want to reduce the amount of sugar or salt.

Guacamole

This is possibly fairly close to the original Aztec dish — avocados and tomatoes as well as chili pepper were common Aztec fare.

~ *1 ripe avocado*

~ *1 small onion, grated*

~ *1 very ripe red tomato, skinned and chopped*

~ *chili powder to taste*

~ *4 tspns olive oil (optional)*

~ *2 tspns lemon or lime juice*

~ *salt and black pepper to taste*

Mash all ingredients together until creamy. Brush with more oil and lemon juice if the dip needs to be kept for a few hours before eating. This stops discoloration. Serve chilled, perhaps sprinkled with a little more chili, or with paprika for color without bite.

MEDICINAL CHILI PEPPER

Mayan Indians used chili pepper for asthma, coughs, sore throats, and respiratory disorders, while Kuna Indians in Panama burned chili pepper with coca to ward off evil spirits. Chili peppers have also been a traditional South American ingredient in pain-killing preparations for thousands of years.

Recent studies have vindicated these traditional uses, indicating that treatment with capsaicin desensitizes the respiratory mucosa to chemical and mechanical irritants. Creams that contain capsaicin have been shown to help about 75 percent of people who suffer neuralgia after a bout of shingles. The "burning feet" syndrome of many diabetics may also be relieved by chili cream.

Chili ointment was also traditionally applied to the painful side of the head during migraines. This does in fact appear to bring some relief; so does sniffing brandy in which chili pepper has been soaked (sniff very, very carefully — pungent chili can blister the inner nostril). It has been claimed

Chili Cold Cure

This is reputed to ward off the onset of a cold by "warming the system." Perhaps it also warns your body that you are serious about not being sick at the moment, and that if it persists, there will be serious and unpleasant consequences. It does make a warming drink if you are cold, wet, and tired, and is even better if you leave out the garlic.

Cover 3 chopped, fresh or dried chili peppers with ½ cup boiling water. Add 1 tspn ginger and 10 cloves crushed garlic. Leave to cool. Add 1 spoonful of mixture to 1 cup warm water with the juice of ½ fresh lemon. Sip slowly. Be prepared to burp long and painfully for several hours after.

Chili Tonic

Cover ½ cup chopped, fresh or dried chili peppers with ½ cup brandy. Seal and leave in a dark place for 3 weeks. Strain and rebottle. Take ½ teaspoonful a day (no more) in 1 cup of warm water as a circulatory tonic.

that chili pepper may ease migraine pain by helping to ease constricted blood vessels.

In the 19th century a couple of drops of chili pepper extract were used to ease toothache. It was also used to stop thumb-sucking and nail-biting — but chili pepper can be very painful on cuticles and under the nails, and this practice is definitely not recommended.

Chili pepper has been hailed as a stimulant for the whole body, increasing blood flow, metabolism, and appetite, and encouraging the sweating so much a part of traditional fever cures. On purely epidemiological evidence, it has been suggested that because many cultures that eat a lot of chili pepper have a low incidence of stomach cancer, anorexia, piles, varicose veins, and liver problems, chili pepper may be of some help in preventing these ailments. However, many of the people of those cultures are also extremely poor, and lack of fat, preservatives, and other affluent extras in their diets may be more relevant than the amount of chili.

Chili pepper, once thought to irritate stomach ulcers, now appears to do no damage. One study of patients with duodenal ulcers showed no difference between those eating a bland diet and those taking 1 g of chili pepper with each meal for four weeks.

Chili Massage Oil

This is a rich, warming oil for when your feet are cold, your back aches, or for rheumatism or arthritis.

Add 1 tbspn chili powder to 2 cups sunflower, olive or linseed oil. I prefer half linseed and half olive oil for deeper penetration. Simmer in a double boiler for 2–3 hours. Cool, strain, and bottle. Keep in a dark place.

Warning: *Never use this oil on broken or sensitive skin. Keep away from eyes, genitals, nipples, and any sunburnt or irritated areas. Test a little first on the back of your hand. If it feels too "hot" after a few minutes, dilute with more oil. Avoid touching the eyes until you have washed your hands well with warm soapy water to which a little vinegar has been added.*

Prairie Oyster

SERVES 1

A reputed hangover cure. It was given to me by a singing teacher to cure laryngitis, while a variation (with orange juice) was given to me after I had my tonsils out. Not recommended except in desperation.

~ *juice of 1 lemon*

~ *1 egg*

~ *dash of Tabasco sauce*

Squeeze the lemon juice into a cup, break in the egg, sprinkle on a few drops of Tabasco, and swallow QUICKLY.

While chili peppers do contain a certain amount of cancer-preventative or anti-tumor substances, none of these occur in large amounts, and most are found plentifully in other common foods. One part of capsaicin has been shown to nullify the mutagenic effects of 6 parts of dimethylnitrosamine — so eating large amounts of chili pepper may negate the cancer-causing nitrosamines found in preserved meats. On the other hand, the same research indicates that capsaicin may be mutagenic itself, or it may precipitate colon cancer. Culinary amounts of chili pepper, however, contain much smaller doses than were experimented with and are therefore quite safe.

Chili pepper is also mildly antibacterial, and makes an excellent gargle for sore throats and laryngitis, preferably combined with other herbs like thyme and lavender. Some alternative diets claim that excluding all solanums from the diet (potatoes, tomatoes, and eggplants as well as chilies) may ease arthritis. On the other hand, regular chili eating may help ease arthritic inflammation. A recent Indian study claims that sweet pepper helps protect the gastric mucosa from ethanol damage.

If all this is confusing, just remember: eating chili pepper is good for you — unless you feel it isn't.

However, there are a few "don'ts" to remember. **Never take large "medicinal" amounts of chili pepper except under medical supervision** — too much chili can lead to liver damage, though it is likely that you would suffer extreme indigestion before that stage. **Never take medicinal doses of chili pepper while pregnant or breastfeeding** (or medicinal doses of any substance that has not been thoroughly tested for its effects on the fetus). Often eating even small amounts of chili pepper while breastfeeding can cause the baby to be irritable, or simply to decide that he or she does not like the taste. **Never use chili seeds medicinally** — they can be toxic in large amounts, though small amounts for culinary purposes are safe.

Chili Ointment

Use this near varicose veins (definitely not on the veins) to encourage blood flow away from them, or on chilblains, as long as the skin isn't broken. It was once used by "pale maidens" to bring color to their cheeks. It works, but can cause blistering and irritation to skin. I don't recommend it.

~ ¼ oz beeswax (use a beeswax candle)

~ ¼ oz anhydrous lanolin (from most drugstores and some supermarkets)

~ 7 tbspns sunflower oil

~ 2 tbspns glycerine (from most supermarkets and drugstores)

~ 5 tbspns water

~ 2 dried chili peppers

Simmer all ingredients in a double boiler for 2 hours. Remove from heat, strain, and pour into jars. If you wish to preserve the cream for more than a few weeks, add 5 drops of benzoin tincture before the mixture cools. Otherwise, keep the cream in the refrigerator.

Chili Goat Cheese

Place chunks of goat cheese in a jar with chopped chili peppers and herbs according to taste — e.g. a sprig of lemon thyme, a little basil, a few bay leaves, or some savory. Fill the jar with olive oil. Leave to marinate in a cool, dark cupboard for at least 1 week before using. This preserve will keep for several months if stored in the refrigerator. Any firm cheese can be used instead of goat cheese.

CHILI PEPPER AND DIETING

There is some argument about just how much chili pepper stimulates the metabolism. A very chili-rich meal will possibly do no more than help you burn up the equivalent of an apple in calories. A study with rats also seems to indicate that capsaicin reduces fat absorption — whether this data is relevant to humans or not is still to be trialed.

Indisputably, however, it is much harder to eat large amounts of chili-laden food than bland food. (A friend once boasted that he could feed ten people with just 2 kidneys in chili sauce, and large amounts of rice to ease the flames.) Chili-laden meals tend to be emphatic and remembered, while a neutral meal of tamer substances is easily forgotten.

Chili pepper also helps promote salivation, which may help digestion.

CHILI PEPPER PESTICIDES

Chili peppers will repel a large number of pests — in fact, any pests that eat leaves or suck sap.

The spray made from chili peppers may be kept for several months in a cool, dark place. Keep it out of the reach of children because of the alcohol content and also because they may gulp it and burn themselves. It is, however, a very safe spray, as few children would take more than one mouthful, and because it repels, rather than kills, pests. Thus it does not harm the predators that may clean up pests naturally in your garden.

CHILI BARNACLE REPELLENT

Chili pepper is reputed to be the basis for a new barnacle repellent paint soon to be marketed, which will have minimal impact on the aquatic environment. (Most commercial barnacle repellents cause severe pollution.) The story goes that a chili lover was eating his lunch on board his boat when he wondered what would happen if he impregnated a bit of wood with chili pepper. So he did. A year later barnacles and other sea life were still avoiding it.

Until this new invention is marketed, keen sailors might try impregnating marine paints, linseed oil and varnishes with chili, to see if they get the same effect.

Quick Chili Pesticide Spray

In an emergency, boil equal amounts of chili pepper and vinegar for 5–10 minutes. Make sure that you leave the lid on while cooking and DON'T SNIFF. Leave to cool, still with the lid on, then strain, and dilute with twice the amount of water.

Chili Pesticide Spray

Soak chili peppers for 2 days to 1 week in either vinegar or, even better, alcohol. Use just enough liquid to cover the chili peppers and make sure that the bottle can be well sealed.

For every 1 part of chili-infused alcohol or vinegar, add 5 parts water and a very little soap to help make it stick to the plant. Spray every few days.

The quantities in the recipe aren't exact because the amount of capsaicin in chili peppers varies — you will need to experiment. The spray, however, must be extremely pungent to be effective.

Chili Garland

This is a wonderful — and very decorative — way to keep your chili peppers. When they have withered on the bush, stand them in the sun for a day or two, then string them on a length of cotton with a darning needle. Hang them in your kitchen where you can pluck one when you need it. Chili peppers hung in this way will last for at least a year, unless the kitchen is very cold and dank.

Chili peppers can also be added to strings of garlic for extra color. Fresh chili peppers can be strung into garlands with bright yellow marigolds for harvest and other fertility festivals.

Chili and Pumpkin Seed Necklace

Wear this for a rustic, homegrown look.

Thread alternating fresh chili peppers and pumpkin seeds onto a long string of cotton. Leave them in the sun or a cool oven to dry.

DECORATIVE CHILI PEPPER

Using chili peppers for decorative purposes may seem a little odd, but their brilliant colors and interesting shapes offer all sorts of possibilities. They can be included in bouquets and garlands of dried flowers, or combined with holly or mistletoe for a Christmas garland on the front door. Instead of candles, wire chili peppers onto the Christmas tree, providing bright, homegrown red "lights" that almost (but not quite) glow in the dark.

SEX AND CHILI

Like many hot or irritating substances, chili pepper has been claimed to be an aphrodisiac, possibly solely because eating an excess amount can lead to genito-urinary irritation, which can be mistaken for sexual excitement. This can result in priapism, an abnormally persistent penal erection, but very little or no pleasure would be associated with it.

According to the *Kama Sutra*, "the drinking of a paste composed of the asparagus raceosmus, the shvadaushtra plant, the guduchi plant, the long pepper [chili pepper] and liquorice, boiled in milk, honey and ghee in the spring" is a prelude to sexual vigor. I haven't tried it.

It has also been claimed that chili pepper increases hormone production, and that the sweat of someone who has eaten lots of chili is unfailingly attractive. This is possibly a theory that only personal experimentation can verify.

Chili peppers have been used not only as a stimulant, but also as a deterrent. Aztec mothers

Chili Mulled Wine

SERVES 4

This is excellent if you are really cold.

~ *4 cups red wine (don't use your best vintage)*

~ *4 red chili peppers, chopped (or to taste)*

~ *2 tbspns packed brown sugar (or to taste)*

~ *2 oranges, sliced*

~ *1 lemon or lime, sliced*

~ *1 tart apple, sliced but not peeled*

~ *6 cloves or ½ tspn cardamom seeds*

~ *1 tspn fresh ginger, chopped*

Combine all ingredients. Heat on the lowest possible heat for at least 20 minutes, stirring occasionally. Drink warm.

Mulled wine is usually less alcoholic than ordinary wine, because the alcohol evaporates. The longer and hotter it is cooked, the less alcohol the mulled wine will contain — but as it is sweet and warming, it is also easy for novices to drink too much of it.

Pineapple and Chili Sherbet

SERVES 4

This is refreshing, with only a faint bite.

~ *1 small and very ripe pineapple (if you can't smell it from a little way off, don't buy it)*
~ *2 fresh red chili peppers*
~ *6 egg whites*
~ *1 cup superfine sugar*

Peel and core the pineapple. Place the pineapple and chili peppers in a blender and purée until smooth. Beat the egg whites until stiff, stir in the sugar and blend very gently with the pineapple purée. Place in a container with a lid in the freezer. Stir at least 3 times as it freezes. Don't let it freeze too solid as the texture won't be as good. If necessary, let it thaw just a little before serving.

Although this sherbet lasts for months if it is kept frozen, it loses the best of its texture and flavor in a few days.

rubbed their daughters' eyes with chili if they gazed at a man shamelessly. Unmarried girls with lustful habits had even more sensitive areas rubbed with it. This would have been excruciating, and may have caused scarring and the permanent deadening of the tissue.

In one study conducted by scientists, the genitalia of water fleas were stimulated by the application of capsaicin. No one thought to ask the fleas, however, whether this stimulation was associated with pain or pleasure.

AND FINALLY: A CHILI PEPPER BOSOM ENHANCER

This recipe comes from a lovely medical reference book from last century, that tells you how to put creosote on syphilitic sores and rub a mixture of opium and soft soap on arthritic limbs.

(I don't recommend either.)

According to the recipe, this mixture will enhance the proportions of your bosom, and "the results will astonish you." A word of warning: if any of this mixture is rubbed on the nipples, the result will certainly be astonishing.

Take 1 cup linseed oil and 1 tbspn cayenne pepper.
Place both in a jar, put the lid on and leave on a warm window sill for 3 weeks, shaking every day.
At the end of that time, strain through 2 layers of cheesecloth, then rub on the area you wish enlarged.

Pineapple Bite

SERVES 4–6

~ 4 cups pineapple juice

~ 1 cup cracked ice

~ 2 cups ginger beer

~ dash of Tabasco sauce

~ fresh mint leaves, shredded

Mix and serve very cold, garnished with mint.

Oranges with Chili

SERVES 4

Don't be put off by the combination of sweetness and chili. If you like hot food, this is wonderful.

~ 6 sweet oranges

~ 2 tspns Cointreau

~ 2 tspns superfine sugar

~ 1 fresh red chili pepper, very finely chopped

Peel the oranges, making sure all pith is removed. Cut them into segments and peel away all membrane. Dissolve the sugar in the Cointreau. Combine the chili with the Cointreau and oranges, and leave to marinate and chill for at least 2 hours. Serve chilled.

ACKNOWLEDGMENTS

Sherringhams Nurseries, North Ryde
Sweet Violets Lindfield, Lindfield

~ ~ ~

PHOTOGRAPHY
Scott Cameron Photography Pty Ltd

FOOD STYLIST
Lisa Hilton

COVER PHOTOGRAPHY
Ivy Hansen